WILDLIFE VIEWING AREAS

Idaho Ecoregions
Northern Rockies
Columbia Plateau
Wasatch and Uinta Mountains
Idaho Batholith
Middle Rockies
Snake River Plain
Northern Basin and Range
Central Basin and Range
Blue Mountains
Wyoming Basin
Lewiston
Boise
Pocatello

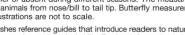

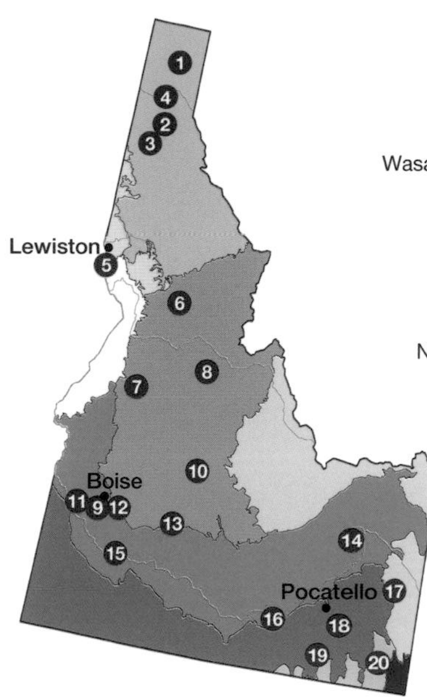

1. Kootenai National Wildlife Refuge (NWR)
2. Farragut State Park
3. Tubbs Hill Nature Park
4. Round Lake State Park
5. Hells Gate State Park
6. Nez Perce National Historical Park
7. Ponderosa State Park
8. Frank Church River of No Return Wilderness
9. Morrison Knudsen Nature Center
10. Sawtooth National Recreation Area
11. Deer Flat NWR
12. Boise River Greenbelt
13. Camas Prairie Centennial Marsh Wildlife Management Area
14. Camas NWR
15. Snake River Birds of Prey National Conservation Area
16. Lake Walcott State Park
17. Grays Lake NWR
18. Cherry Springs Nature Area
19. Curlew National Grassland
20. Bear Lake NWR

Most illustrations show the adult male in breeding coloration. Colors and markings may be duller or absent during different seasons. The measurements denote the length of animals from nose/bill to tail tip. Butterfly measurements denote wingspan. Illustrations are not to scale.

Made in the USA

Waterford Press publishes reference guides that introduce readers to nature observation, outdoor recreation and survival skills. Product information is featured on the website: **www.waterfordpress.com**

 To order or for information on custom published products please call 800-434-2555 or email orderdesk@waterfordpress.com. For permissions or to share comments email editor@waterfordpress.com.

ISBN 978-1-58355-626-9 $7.95 U.S.
50795
9 781583 556269
UPC 8 84682 00997 7
10 9 8 7 6 5 4 3 2 1 2213603

IDAHO WILDLIFE – A Folding Pocket Guide to Familiar Animals

WATERFORD PRESS

A POCKET NATURALIST® GUIDE

IDAHO WILDLIFE

A Folding Pocket Guide to Familiar Animals

T0123951

INSECTS

Millipede
Order Diplopoda
To 5 in. (13 cm)
Has 2 pairs of legs per body segment.

Common House Centipede
Order Chilopoda
To 5 in. (13 cm)
Has a single pair of legs per segment and long antennae. Can inflict a painful bite.

Wood Tick
Dermacentor spp.
To .25 in. (.6 cm)
Feeds on blood and drops off when full. Can transmit diseases.

Black-and-yellow Garden Spider
Argiope aurantia
To 1.25 in. (3.2 cm)

Goldenrod Crab Spider
Misumena vatia
To .4 in. (1 cm)

Northern Bluet
Enallagma annexum
To 1.5 in. (4 cm)
Like most damselflies, it rests with its wings closed.

American Emerald
Cordulia shurtleffii
To 2 in. (5 cm)
Eyes are bright green. Like most dragonflies, it rests with its wings open.

Ladybug Beetle
Family Coccinellidae
To .5 in. (1.3 cm)
Red wing covers are black-spotted.

Red Damsel
Amphiagrion abbreviatum
To 1 in. (3 cm)

Four-spotted Skimmer
Libellula quadrimaculata
To 1.75 in (4.5
Wings have a small dark spot at their midpoint.

Colorado Potato Beetle
Leptinotarsa decimlineata
To .5 in. (1.3 cm)
Garden pest is one of over 1,400 species of leaf-eating beetles.

Bumble Bee
Bombus spp.
To 1 in. (3 cm)
Stout, furry bee is large and noisy.

Honey Bee
Apis mellifera
To .75 in. (2 cm)
Slender bee has pollen baskets on its rear legs. Can only sting once.

Yellow Jacket
Vespula pensylvanica
To .63 in. (1.6 cm)
Aggressive picnic pest can sting repeatedly.

Whirligig Beetle
Gyrinus spp.
To .5 in. (1.3 cm)
Large swarms swirl around together on the water's surface.

Water Strider
Gerris spp.
To .5 in. (1.3 cm)
Long-legged insect skates along the water's surface.

BUTTERFLIES & MOTHS

Pale Tiger Swallowtail
Pterourus eurymedon
To 4 in. (10 cm)

Monarch
Danaus plexippus
To 4 in. (10 cm)
Idaho's state insect.

Western Tiger Swallowtail
Papilio rutulus
To 4 in. (10 cm)

Western Tailed Blue
Cupido amyntula
To 1.25 in. (3.2 cm)
Note orange mark above tail on hindwings.

Painted Lady
Vanessa cardui
To 2.5 in. (6 cm)
Tip of forewing is dark with white spots.

Cabbage White
Pieris rapae
To 2 in. (5 cm)
One of the most common butterflies.

Red Admiral
Vanessa atalanta
To 2.5 in. (6 cm)

Orange Sulphur
Colias eurytheme
To 2.5 in. (6 cm)
Gold-orange butterfly has a prominent forewing spot.

Sara Orangetip
Anthocharis sara
To 1.5 in. (4 cm)

Spring Azure
Celastrina ladon
To 1.3 in. (3.6 cm)
One of the earliest spring butterflies.

Mourning Cloak
Nymphalis antiopa
To 3.5 in. (9 cm)
Emerges during the first spring thaw.

Milbert's Tortoiseshell
Aglais milberti
To 2 in. (5 cm)

White-lined Sphinx
Hyles lineata
To 3.5 in. (9 cm)
Active at all hours, it hovers like a hummingbird.

Sheep Moth
Hemileuca eglanterina
To 3 in. (8 cm)
Common in pastures and meadows.

Bumblebee Moth
Hemaris diffinis
To 2 in. (5 cm)
Distinguished by clear wings and furry body.

FISHES

Cutthroat Trout
Oncorhynchus clarkii To 39 in. (98 cm)
Told by red mark near throat.
Idaho's state fish.

Rainbow Trout
Oncorhynchus mykiss To 44 in. (1.1 m)

Brown Trout
Salmo trutta To 40 in. (1 m)
Has red and black spots on its body.

Lake Trout
Salvelinus namaycush To 4 ft. (1.2 m)
Tail is deeply forked.

Smallmouth Bass
Micropterus dolomieu To 27 in. (68 cm)
Jaw joint is beneath the eye.

Brook Trout
Salvelinus fontinalis To 28 in. (70 cm)
Reddish side spots have blue halos.

Largemouth Bass
Micropterus salmoides To 40 in. (1 m)
Jaw joint extends past eye.

Common Carp
Cyprinus carpio To 30 in. (75 cm)
Introduced species has an arched back and mouth barbels.

Sockeye (Red) Salmon
Oncorhynchus nerka To 33 in. (83 cm)
Red breeding male has hooked jaws and a green head. Native to central Idaho.

Crappie
Pomoxis spp. To 16 in. (40 cm)

Yellow Perch
Perca flavescens To 16 in. (40 cm)

Pumpkinseed
Lepomis gibbosus To 16 in. (40 cm)

Walleye
Sander vitreus To 40 in. (1 m)
Note white spot on lower lobe of tail.

Channel Catfish
Ictalurus punctatus To 4 ft. (1.2 m)
Note prominent 'whiskers.'

Mountain Whitefish
Prosopium williamsoni To 22 in. (55 cm)
Common in alpine lakes and streams.

REPTILES & AMPHIBIANS

Boreal Toad
Anaxyrus boreas
To 4 in. (10 cm)
Note cream-colored dorsal stripe. Males have a soft, clucking call.

Northern Leopard Frog
Lithobates pipiens
To 4 in. (10 cm)
Brown to green frog has dark spots on its back. Call is a rattling snore with grunts and moans.

Western Chorus Frog
Pseudacris triseriata
To 1.5 in. (4 cm)
Note dark stripes on back. Call sounds like running a thumbnail over the teeth of a comb.

Tiger Salamander
Ambystoma mavortium
To 13 in. (33 cm)
Pattern of yellowish and dark blotches is variable.

Short-horned Lizard
Phrynosoma douglasii To 6 in. (15 cm)
Head is covered with spines. S. Idaho.

Western Skink
Plestiodon skiltonianus
To 9 in. (23 cm)
Juveniles have bright blue tails.

Painted Turtle
Chrysemys picta To 10 in. (25 cm)
N. Idaho.

Collared Lizard
Crotaphytus collaris To 14 in. (35 cm)
Note 2 dark collar markings. S. Idaho.

Sagebrush Lizard
Sceloporus graciosus
To 6 in. (15 cm)
Note red-orange spot behind foreleg and blue belly. S. Idaho.

Rubber Boa
Charina bottae To 33 in. (83 cm)
Glossy, stout gray to brown snake.

Western Terrestrial Garter Snake
Thamnophis elegans elegans
To 40 in. (1 m)

Northern Water Snake
Nerodia sipedon To 4.5 ft. (1.4 m)
Note dark blotches on back.

Valley Garter Snake
Thamnophis sirtalis fitchi
To 4 ft. (1.2 m)

Great Basin Gopher Snake
Pituophis catenifer deserticola
To 8 ft. (2.4 m)
Thick-bodied, barred snake.

Western Rattlesnake
Crotalus viridis To 5 ft. (1.5 m)
Venomous snake has a spade-shaped head. Found at elevations below 10,000 ft. (3000 m).

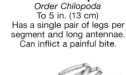

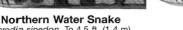

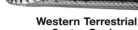

Canada Goose
Branta canadensis
To 45 in. (1.14 m)

Trumpeter Swan
Cygnus buccinator
To 6 ft. (1.8 m)
Note stout black bill.

Sandhill Crane
Antigone canadensis
To 4 ft. (1.2 m)
Grays Lake NWR
hosts the world's
largest concentration
of breeding birds.

Mallard
Anas platyrhynchos
To 28 in. (70 cm)

Great Blue Heron
Ardea herodias
To 4.5 ft. (1.4 m)

American Wigeon
Mareca americana
To 23 in. (58 cm)

Killdeer
Charadrius vociferus
To 12 in. (30 cm)
Note two
breast bands.

Peregrine Falcon
Falco peregrinus
To 20 in. (50 cm)
Idaho's state raptor.

Bald Eagle
Haliaeetus leucocephalus
To 40 in. (1 m)

American Kestrel
Falco sparverius
To 12 in. (30 cm)

Red-tailed Hawk
Buteo jamaicensis
To 25 in. (63 cm)

Prairie Falcon
Falco mexicanus
To 17 in. (43 cm)
Note dark 'armpits.'

Rufous Hummingbird
Selasphorus rufus
To 3.5 in. (9 cm)

Black-chinned Hummingbird
Archilochus alexandri
To 3.5 in. (9 cm)

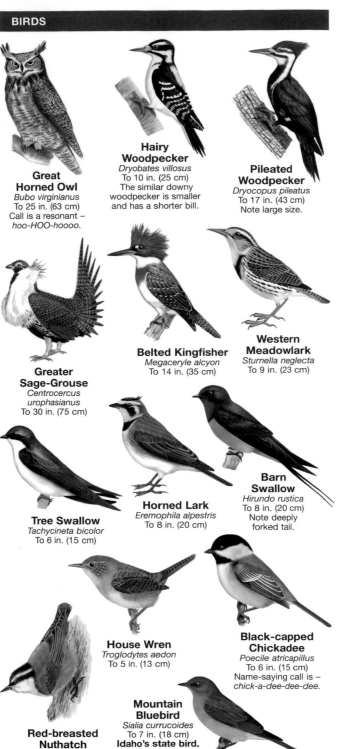

Great Horned Owl
Bubo virginianus
To 25 in. (63 cm)
Call is a resonant–
hoo-HOO-hoooo.

Hairy Woodpecker
Dryobates villosus
To 10 in. (25 cm)
The similar downy
woodpecker is smaller
and has a shorter bill.

Pileated Woodpecker
Dryocopus pileatus
To 17 in. (43 cm)
Note large size.

Greater Sage-Grouse
Centrocercus urophasianus
To 30 in. (75 cm)

Belted Kingfisher
Megaceryle alcyon
To 14 in. (35 cm)

Western Meadowlark
Sturnella neglecta
To 9 in. (23 cm)

Tree Swallow
Tachycineta bicolor
To 6 in. (15 cm)

Horned Lark
Eremophila alpestris
To 8 in. (20 cm)

Barn Swallow
Hirundo rustica
To 8 in. (20 cm)
Note deeply
forked tail.

Red-breasted Nuthatch
Sitta canadensis
To 4.5 in. (11 cm)

House Wren
Troglodytes aedon
To 5 in. (13 cm)

Mountain Bluebird
Sialia currucoides
To 7 in. (18 cm)
Idaho's state bird.

Black-capped Chickadee
Poecile atricapillus
To 6 in. (15 cm)
Name-saying call is –
chick-a-dee-dee-dee.

Canada Jay
Perisoreus canadensis
To 14 in. (35 cm)

Steller's Jay
Cyanocitta stelleri
To 14 in. (35 cm)

Western Tanager
Piranga ludoviciana
To 7 in. (18 cm)

Red-winged Blackbird
Agelaius phoeniceus
To 9 in. (23 cm)

Black-billed Magpie
Pica hudsonia
To 22 in. (55 cm)

European Starling
Sturnus vulgaris
To 8 in. (20 cm)

American Crow
Corvus brachyrhynchos
To 22 in. (55 cm)
Call is a distinct – caw.

Common Raven
Corvus corax
To 27 in. (68 cm)
Call is a hoarse croak.

American Robin
Turdus migratorius
To 11 in. (28 cm)

Cedar Waxwing
Bombycilla cedrorum
To 7 in. (18 cm)
Red wing marks look
like waxy droplets.

House Finch
Haemorhous mexicanus
To 6 in. (15 cm)

Yellow Warbler
Setophaga petechia
To 5 in. (13 cm)

Dark-eyed Junco
Junco hyemalis
To 7 in. (18 cm)

American Goldfinch
Spinus tristis
To 5 in. (13 cm)

House Sparrow
Passer domesticus
To 6 in. (15 cm)

Little Brown Bat
Myotis lucifugus
To 3.5 in. (9 cm)

American Pika
Ochotona princeps
To 9 in. (23 cm)
Inhabits rock piles in
mountainous areas.

Snowshoe Hare
Lepus americanus
To 20 in. (50 cm)
Coat is white in winter.

White-tailed Jackrabbit
Lepus townsendii
To 26 in. (65 cm)
Note large ears
and white tail.

Mountain Cottontail
Sylvilagus nuttallii
To 16 in. (40 cm)

Deer Mouse
Peromyscus maniculatus
To 8 in. (20 cm)
Distinguished
by its white
undersides and
hairy tail.

Least Chipmunk
Neotamias minimus
To 9 in. (23 cm)
Note white stripes
on side and face.

Meadow Vole
Microtus pennsylvanicus
To 7 in. (18 cm)
Small mouse-like
creature has long
fur and a short tail.

Red Squirrel
Tamiasciurus hudsonicus
To 14 in. (35 cm)
Coat is rusty red above
and whitish below.

Fox Squirrel
Sciurus niger
To 28 in. (70 cm)
Note large size and
bushy tail. Largest
squirrel in the U.S.
Introduced in
several locations.

Golden-mantled Ground Squirrel
Callospermophilus lateralis
To 12 in. (30 cm)

Common Muskrat
Ondatra zibethicus To 2 ft. (60 cm)
Aquatic rodent has a naked, scaly tail.

Long-tailed Weasel
Mustela frenata
To 21 in. (53 cm)

Common Porcupine
Erethizon dorsatum
To 3 ft. (90 cm)
Large rodent has barbed
quills near its rear that it
uses for defense.

Yellow-bellied Marmot
Marmota flaviventris
To 28 in. (70 cm)

Hoary Marmot
Marmota caligata
To 32 in. (80 cm)

American Beaver
Castor canadensis
To 4 ft. (1.2 m)

American Badger
Taxidea taxus
To 35 in. (88 cm)

Striped Skunk
Mephitis mephitis
To 32 in. (80 cm)

Common Raccoon
Procyon lotor To 40 in. (1 m)

Mink
Neovison vison
To 28 in. (70 cm)
Chin is white.

Bobcat
Lynx rufus
To 4 ft. (1.2 m)

Northern River Otter
Lontra canadensis
To 52 in. (1.3 m)

Red Fox
Vulpes vulpes
To 40 in. (1 m)

Coyote
Canis latrans To 52 in. (1.3 m)

Gray Wolf
Canis lupus To 6.5 ft. (2 m)
Coat color is usually gray,
but black, white and mottled
variants exist. Populations are
recovering in N. Idaho.

Mountain Goat
Oreamnos americanus
To 6 ft. (1.8 m)

Mountain Lion
Puma concolor To 9 ft. (2.7 m)

Pronghorn
Antilocapra americana
To 5 ft. (1.5 m)

Bighorn Sheep
Ovis canadensis
To 6 ft. (1.8 m)

White-tailed Deer
Odocoileus virginianus
To 7 ft. (2.1 m)
Fluffy tail is white below.

Mule Deer
Odocoileus hemionus To 7.5 ft. (2.3 m)
Rope-like tail is black-tipped.

Moose
Alces alces To 10 ft. (3 m)

Elk
Cervus canadensis
To 10 ft. (3 m)

Grizzly Bear
Ursus arctos horribilis To 7 ft. (2.1 m)
Large brownish bear has a prominent
shoulder hump and a 'dished' face.
Populations are recovering in N. Idaho.

Black Bear
Ursus americanus
To 6 ft. (1.8 m)
Coat color ranges from
black to brown.